My Eyes

DARE TO BELIEVE

Bridget P. Robinson, M.A.

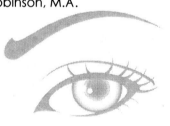

MAC Publishing

Printed in the United States of America

First Printing, 2015

Published by:
MAC Publishing
www.macpub.org

MY EYES DARE TO BELIEVE
ISBN-10: 0990963462
ISBN-13: 978-0-9909634-6-2

TABLE OF CONTENTS

FOREWORD

Minister Bridget Robinson is a born again Christian and an excellent example of God's "favor." Her trials and tribulations through her lifetime have anchored her spirit, mind and soul. They did not break her! Through the prompting of the Holy Spirit she has triumphed through domestic violence, broken relationships, damaged health and emotional anger and pain. She has lived to tell it while hoping that those who share her same story will be encouraged to take off the façade and face what she thought would never end.

I graciously applaud her for her boldness and desire to conquer everything that got in her way as she struggled to find her self-worth and confidence in situations that seemingly had no end. In the pages of this book you will find basic truths to enable you to live and love courageously, joyously, and be at peace with yourself.

Bridget refuses to feel resentment, nor does she harbor any animosity, because she knows through it all, the Lord was her strength. She is a spirit-filled woman walking in her destiny, embracing her new beginnings, and realizing that she was born to win!

-Minister Carol Owens Ford

ACKNOWLEDGEMENTS

To my children, Hadassah Vashti Fleming and Jeffery Alexander Fleming, Jr., thanks for being my reason for breaking the chains of abuse. Hadassah, the first time I looked into your eyes you became my "anchor of hope" – hope for a better tomorrow. My inspiration for making courageous steps was birthed through you, and my beloved son, Jeffery. Holding the two of you in my arms gave me the strength to face my tomorrows and step boldly into my future. I love you so much. You are the wind beneath my wings!

To Jeffery, you inspired me and pushed me to write the book and adhere to a timeline. You held me accountable to what God has called me to do. Thanks for believing in me and pushing me to stay the course although rocky. I remember you saying to me, "Mom, it's amazing to see you go from writing 1 page to 47 pages. Keep going." Little did I know at the time, I was making strides. You were watching me grow each time as you spoke life to me. I love you and thank God for you being a noble son.

To Nehemiah Alexander McPherson, my grandson, you are my refreshment. You replenish me. Your birth is symbolic of God's birthing of my ministry. Holding you in my arms and watching you grow is a continual oasis of joy. I love you so much.

To my spiritual father, Bishop Alfred A. Owens, Jr., thank you for having "Bread" in the city. When I arrived at the doorsteps of Greater Mount Calvary Holy Church I was famished. I was extremely hungry for the Word of God. Not only did you feed me as my Shepherd, you became my spiritual father. Thanks for providing me with a safe place to heal emotionally and grow spiritually. Thanks for your gentle words of encouragement, support, and for believing in me. I love you.

To my spiritual mother, Co-Pastor Susie C. Owens, thanks for all of your prayers for my family and I. Thanks for the transformational conversations and supporting my family and I during difficult times. Thank you for challenging me in your signature class: Women in Ministry. You stared me directly in the face and with your voice of authority you said, "You've got to know that you know what God called you to do." You made me speak truth to power and proclaim my identity in God. I love you so much and I pray to God that I will never make you ashamed. I love you.

To my dearest friend, Carol Owens Ford (Minister), you helped me to pick up the broken pieces of my life. Thanks for going before me and letting me know God is able to put the pieces of my life back together again. You have worn many hats in my life: auntie, mother, life coach and mentor. Thank you for your life-changing words, for allowing me to cry, share, and just be me. Thanks for the many hours you dedicated to me birthing out my first book. I thank God for you taking the time out of your busy schedule to read, edit, and advise what God has allowed me to share with the world through my testimony. I love you.

To Elder Jacqueline Rice, I love you. I'm so thankful to Bishop Owens for bringing us together. Christian counseling works. You have been instrumental in my life and family. Thanks for allowing us to keep it real.

To Elder Lisa Jackson and Evangelist Desiree Marshall, your witness is genuine. It's remarkable how God places people in your path to direct you back to Him when you have lost your way. On my wilderness journey back to Jesus, our paths crossed. You took time to share the good news when I was lost in a strange land and angry with God. Your light in my world of darkness directed my footsteps to the doors of the church. Life lesson learned: Never miss an opportunity to witness to a lost soul. You will always have a special place in my heart. I love you.

To Roger David Robinson, Sr., you are the only natural father I have ever known. You chose to love me and make me your namesake. I love you. To my brothers, David Robinson, we will always be "Two of a Kind", and Kendal Woods, my prayer is for you to always believe in yourself. To my dearest cousin, Purvis Scott, thanks for being my superman. Here you come to save the day! I love you. To my family, thanks for all of your prayers.

To my friends, you know who you are. We are older now and our lives have taken different paths; however, our love keeps us going. I have learned that friends come into your life for a reason, a season, and some for a lifetime. Whatever category you may find yourself, you made a difference in my life and I pray I made an impact in yours.

To Marcus Inabinet, my beloved "snowflake" and to all other snowflakes, I pray our strength in the Lord as we continue our fight against Sarcoidosis as we "Dare to Believe."

DEDICATION

My mother is a courageous, humble woman of faith. My mother has taught me many life lessons that have sustained me as I walk down the unpredictable road called life. My mother has gone before me managing the task of single parenting and chronic illness. In spite of her lifetime bouts of depression and bipolar episodes she has always placed the welfare of my brothers and me first, always ensuring we had a roof over our head, clothes, and food to eat. I remember the days when my mother did not eat so we could eat. I remember the days when she worked her faith through prayer and fasting and we witnessed God's divine hand of protection, provision and promises be fulfilled.

My mother handles her mental illness with dignity and grace. In and out of treatment she never gave up her faith that God has healed her and is healing her. My mother doesn't look like what she has been through. My mother's prayer life is what has kept us from seen and unseen dangers. I remember waking up in the middle of the night and finding my mother praying and/or singing to the Most High God. This was not a one-time occurring event; it was the norm.

My mother loved us so much that she introduced us to her God, Jesus Christ, by taking us to church faithfully during the week. She also set aside time to pray as a family every Saturday evening and maintained an atmosphere of praise and worship. The best gifts my mother could have ever given me were her faith in God and a praying spirit. Because she laid the foundation of my Christian walk, I'm able to stand against the wiles of the enemy and trust God in spite of what my eyes have seen and dare to believe.

I dedicate my first book to my mother, Beverly Arlene Robinson.

I am because she is.

Bridget P. Robinson,
Birth of a Prayer Warrior

CHAPTER ONE:
Do You See What I See?

Alone in the bathtub I sat, nothing but skin and bones. There I withered away wondering what was wrong with me. I was too tired to breathe on my own; somehow magically I continued to circulate air through what felt like two dried up lungs. The adipose tissue evaporated from underneath my skin, and my skin draped lightly over my rib cage. I could count each rib one by one from the outside in. I saw strange wiggly lines moving back and forth in my eyes. My eyes burned and hurt. They were reddish-pink and so sensitive to the light I could barely open my eyelids. All I wanted as I sat in that big white bathtub that swallowed me up was for my mother to notice that her daughter was being eaten up.

I was 17 years old. It was my senior year of high school. It was my time to shine, my time for lights, cameras, and center stage. My physique was: 5'7, 110 lbs., size C cup bra, medium length hair, mocha brown skin, coke bottle shape, a virgin saving myself for marriage and a Christian. Simply put: I was beautiful from the inside out. I had worked hard for this moment academically and socially. Throughout my high school preparation at C. A. Johnson High School, I participated actively in the following student activities:

AIR ROTC
AIR ROTC Drill Team
Concert Band
Drama Club
Marching Band
Pep Club
Student Council

But the "STOP" sign came hurdling at my sight and brought everything to a screeching halt. Do you see what I see?

I was losing weight fast and it didn't matter how much I ate, I couldn't hold any food on my stomach. From the moment food entered into my mouth and down to my stomach I passed it through my digestive track like liquid. I went straight to the toilet. My stomach hurt and my intestines contracted violently. I had pain running up and down my legs from my stomach. I was scared. I was losing weight suddenly. I was thin, too thin, skinny sick.

My skin was changing too. I had patches of red raised bumps on my legs like in a circle pattern. My hair was also falling out. I had severe night sweats and chills. I was a hot mess. All of this was happening right around the end of the first and beginning of the second school semester in 1988.

As I walked around from day to day my world became more and more difficult to navigate because the sunlight or any ray of light had become so sensitive to my eyes that I began to mimic the behavior of the famous gremlins when they came into contact with sunlight shouting, "Light! Light! Light!" However, I was unable to see that destruction was heading my way.

My world was changing so fast and people were beginning to notice my drastic physical changes such as my friends, classmates, and teachers; however, the people that mattered most to me my mother and my oldest brother didn't even notice. My outward symptoms were so apparent to others that a few of my classmates approached my brother and asked him if I had AIDS. AIDS was the main headliner of the day from politics, religion, and health.

My computer teacher also noticed that I had lost a lot of weight and was wasting away. My eyes were very weak and reddish pink. With her discerning eyes on me, and watching me closely for a period of time she was very much concerned about me. Finally, she got right up in my personal space during instructional time and asked me the private dirty little secret question, "Are you anorexic?"

At that time culturally, I was surprised that my computer teacher ask me this thought-provoking question that could potentially give an explanation for my sudden weight loss and physical changes that she had observed. In the late 1980's anorexia was not a social illness that drew attention to black girls. Primarily white girls were coping with the eating disorder, so the question was awkward because it was solicited from my computer teacher and she was white.

A white teacher asking a black student if she was anorexic sounded strange to me. At least at the time in my world it did. She told me to go to the school nurse to be evaluated. The teacher gave me a hall pass and down the hall I went scared at not having an answer as to why my body was falling apart.

The school nurse did a complete examination of my fragile body from head to toe. From her assessment she deduced that I could have the "pinkeye" or medically termed *conjunctivitis*. I was given a letter to take home to my mother informing her that I could not return back to school until an eye doctor saw me and cleared me to return to school.

Nervous and anxious I went home with the nurse's note to give to my mother. My mother quickly notified me that she wasn't going to be able to take off from work to take me to the eye doctor and gave very clear instructions that no one was to call her job; that included the eye doctor. Basically, I was on my own. This also included finding an eye doctor (ophthalmologist) and taking myself to the appointment.

I ran my fingers through the yellow pages of the phone book. I found an eye doctor's office that was close to my house and I made the appointment. I took the bus and walked a few blocks. My eyes ached and the sunlight made it difficult to walk down the street with my head lifted up. As I approached the medical building, I realized that I was all alone. No one was with me. I was scared, sad, and I felt abandoned. Then, I remembered Psalm 27:10, which says, *"when my father and my mother forsake me, then the LORD will take me up."* I learned at an early age how to pray, and I always felt close to God especially when I felt alone.

As a new patient, I completed the medical paperwork as best I could, and I attached the school nurse's note. I waited patiently for my name to be called. Finally, when my name was called I got up and followed the nurse. As I entered the examination room, the doctor asked where my parents were, I informed him that I was there by myself and my mother was unable to make it because she had to work.

The eye exam was intense. The eye doctor asked a lot of questions. The eye doctor dilated my eyes and examined my eyes from every possible angle. Then he pulled out his wooden case full of different types of handheld lenses. He precisely took notes and was astonished and full of bewilderment at the same time. The examination took all day. I even had a break for lunch. Upon his completion of the examination and assessment, he stated he needed to speak with my parents. With much concern and appearing to be agitated, he asked me why I came to this visit all by myself. The doctor needed to speak with my mother. I told him he could not call my mother's job because I was given direct instructions from my mother not to call. The doctor stated that he could not release me from his medical practice until he had spoken to a responsible adult.

Who could I call? I felt trapped. Who could the eye doctor talk to that would understand his findings and would be able to explain it to my mother? I thought about my mother's sister who is a nurse and I gave the doctor her telephone number. The doctor called her job. However, he was not able to get through the first time. He left a message and I had to wait. Yes, I waited back in the patient waiting area until my aunt connected with the eye doctor. I had a morning appointment, but I did not leave the doctor's office until near the close of business.

The doctor explained his findings to my aunt; what I had was not "pinkeye" but was something more serious medically that not yet had been discovered and diagnosed. He stated that I urgently needed to be seen by my pediatrician. I was seriously sick.

Finally, I was seen with my symptoms. I was no longer lurking in the dark shadows fading away. My computer teacher, my school nurse, and the eye doctor saw a young lady who needed someone to advocate for her. Do you see what I see? Me...

CHAPTER TWO
Sarcoidosis: A Kaleidoscope

My mother took off from work with much hesitation. She did the motherly thing considering other responsible adults at this critical juncture were peeping slightly into our closet of domestic affairs. There was pressure to perform her motherly duties. And, for a brief moment in time she noticed me and my need for medical attention. Her daughter had withered away.

We arrived at the prestigious Children's Medical Center located in Columbia, South Carolina, a hospital on the cutting edge of medical treatment and research for children. I was nervous and scared as my mother and I walked from the bus stop to the wide glass entrance doors that motioned to open according to our forward syncopated steps. Moving forward towards medical answers to unlock the mystery as to why my teenage world was falling apart.

Before the physician started his medical examination of my skinny, fragile body he asked a series of health questions. He wanted to document every detail to ensure he could begin to hypothesize a potential diagnosis. I provided the physician with the detailed doctor's notes from the ophthalmologist. At the youthful age of 18, I had to begin to advocate for myself. My mother was physically there. However, she was just a figment of my imagination because she had no idea of my symptoms. I had all the answers to the medical questions as to when I began to experience these life-changing symptoms:

- *Red, teary eyes and blurred vision*
- *Weight loss*
- *Night sweats*
- *Persistent dry cough*
- *Fatigue*
- *Shortness of breath*
- *Tender reddish butterfly patches on my leg*
- *Swollen and painful joints*
- *Pain in the hands and feet*

The physician began to examine me with tender hands of curiosity. As he continued to run his hands over my body, his fingers encountered enlarged and tender lymph glands in my neck, armpits, and groin. He examined my lower limbs and noticed a rash on both of my legs and raised skin with a butterfly pattern. The pattern was classic at first glance to Lupus. A hypothesis was beginning to emerge. A biopsy of the skin rash was imperative because it would yield much needed confirmation of a diagnosis. The biopsy was done and the pending results would be revealed in seven days.

The physician ordered a battery of blood tests. The lab results indicated I had a serious autoimmune disease, but what was it? More tests were ordered and also a chest x-ray. The chest x-ray revealed enlarged lymph glands in the chest and around the lungs.

After collection of the preliminary test results the examining physician and the medical team recommended hospitalization until they had a diagnosis, because the autoimmune disease was systemic and aggressive treatment was needed right away. My whole body was attacking itself with internal destruction that had manifested itself outside for the whole world to see.

Staying in the hospital was not an option for me. I knew I needed treatment but I could not stay in the hospital. I had too much responsibility. It was my senior year in high school. I had a job, and I watched over and took care of my young brother. I couldn't believe what I was hearing. Hospitalization!!! No way. How could I? I had to convince my physician who had become my doctor and the treatment team to let me go home. There wasn't a diagnosis yet; however, treatment was of the essence. The course of treatment was to begin immunosuppressive therapy. My doctor wanted to monitor the physical impact of starting the treatment.

My maturity was evident throughout the day because I was able to effectively communicate with my doctor and treatment team. It was determined that I was dependable enough to be released into my own care. I promised I would follow my treatment regimen and keep all my appointments. Little did I know that my world was becoming a kaleidoscope, patterns of unpredictable changes and events.

The biopsy result confirmed: Sarcoidosis not Lupus. The eye condition diagnosed by Columbia Eye Center: Uveitis. The scene just shifted.

I had become akin to the woman in the Bible with the "Issue of Blood" and the blind man at the pool of

Bethesda. These two Bible characters had become a foreshadow of things to come.

Primary Diagnosis:
Sarcoidosis - Sarcoidosis is a disease in which inflammation occurs in the lymph nodes, lungs, liver, eyes, skin, or other tissues. It causes the development of granulomas. Granulomas are masses resembling little tumors. They are made up of clumps of cells from the immune system. **There is no cure for Sarcoidosis.**

Woman with the Issue of Blood:
Luke 8:43-48 Amplified Bible (AMP)

43 And a woman who had suffered from a flow of blood for twelve years and had spent all her living upon physicians, and could not be healed by anyone,

44 Came up behind Him and touched the fringe of His garment, and immediately her flow of blood ceased.

45 And Jesus said, Who is it who touched Me? When all were denying it, Peter and those who were with him said, Master, the multitudes surround You and press You on every side!

46 But Jesus said, Someone did touch Me; for I perceived that [healing] power has gone forth from Me.

47 And when the woman saw that she had not escaped notice, she came up trembling, and, falling down before Him, she declared in the presence of all the people for what reason she had touched Him and how she had been instantly cured.

48 And He said to her, Daughter, your faith (your confidence and trust in Me) has made you well! Go (enter) [ᵇ]into peace (untroubled, undisturbed well-being).

Eye Diagnosis:

Uveitis (u-ve-i-tis) - is inflammation of the uvea, the middle layer of the eye. The uvea consists of the iris, choroid and ciliary body. The choroid is sandwiched between the retina and the white of the eye (sclera), and it provides blood flow to the deep layers of the retina. **<u>Uveitis can lead to permanent vision loss and there is no cure.</u>**

<u>Blind Man at the Pool of Bethesda:</u>
John 5:1-15 Amplified Bible (AMP)

1 Later on there was a Jewish festival (feast) for which Jesus went up to Jerusalem.

2 Now there is in Jerusalem a pool near the Sheep Gate. This pool in the Hebrew is called Bethesda, having five porches (alcoves, colonnades, doorways).

3 In these lay a great number of sick folk—some blind, some crippled, and some paralyzed (shriveled up)—[ᵃ]waiting for the bubbling up of the water.

4 For an angel of the Lord went down at appointed seasons into the pool and moved and stirred up the water; whoever then first, after the stirring up of the water, stepped in was cured of whatever disease with which he was afflicted.

5 There was a certain man there who had suffered with a deep-seated and lingering disorder for thirty-eight years.

6 When Jesus noticed him lying there [helpless], knowing that he had already been a long time in that condition, He said to him, Do you want to become well? [Are you really in earnest about getting well?]

7 The invalid answered, Sir, I have nobody when the water is moving to put me into the pool; but while I am trying to come [into it] myself, somebody else steps down ahead of me.

8 Jesus said to him, Get up! Pick up your bed (sleeping pad) and walk!

9 Instantly the man became well and recovered his strength and picked up his bed and walked. But that happened on the Sabbath.

10 So the Jews kept saying to the man who had been healed, It is the Sabbath, and you have no right to pick up your bed [it is not lawful].

11 He answered them, The [b]Man Who healed me and gave me back my strength, He Himself said to me, Pick up your bed and walk!

12 They asked him, Who is the Man Who told you, Pick up your bed and walk?

13 Now the invalid who had been healed did not know who it was, for Jesus had quietly gone away [had passed on unnoticed], since there was a crowd in the place.

14 Afterward, when Jesus found him in the temple, He said to him, See, you are well! Stop sinning or something worse may happen to you.

15 The man went away and told the Jews that it was Jesus Who had made him well.

Chapter Three
Jehovah Jireh - The Lord My Provider

Genesis 22:14 Amplified Bible (AMP)

¹⁴ So Abraham called the name of that place The Lord Will Provide. And it is said to this day, On the mount of the Lord it will be provided.

Lamenting over my dual diagnosis of Sarcoidosis and Uveitis I was left on my own to determine how I was going to pay for the frequent visits to the doctors and my medications. I had a part-time job working at Family Dollar as a cashier making a minimum wage of $3.25 per hour, and I had no medical insurance.

I was impoverished. I was on the brink of falling through the cracks of the healthcare system because my small pocket was penniless. I needed the LORD to provide. I remember my mother quoting, Psalm 37:25, "I have been young and now am old, yet have I not seen the [uncompromisingly] righteous forsaken or their seed begging bread" (AMP). I did not know how, but I knew God was going to provide for me.

I contacted the Department of Social Services and made an appointment with a social worker to apply for medical assistance. After review of my finances and demographics it was determined that I was not eligible for Medicaid. I had aged out of Medicaid at the age of 18, and I had no children. Also, I was not old enough to receive Medicare. Therefore, with my limited income I was left with paying the total cost of my healthcare expenses out of pocket.

Feeling stressed and desperately lonely, I wondered how I was going to make it. I was still in high school and my take home pay from my part-time job only covered my basic needs. I had no human flesh that I could count on to help me financially or emotionally.

Proverbs 18:24 Amplified Bible (AMP)

24 The man of many friends [a friend of all the world] will prove himself a bad friend, but there is a friend who sticks closer than a brother.

That friend was God. I had to believe that God would provide, and He did! I was referred to a non-profit organization, Medical Charities. Medical Charities provided me with a security blanket, they paid 70% of my medical expenses and negotiated with my medical providers for me to receive medical services on a sliding scale. God's Word became active in my life.

Luke 12:7 Amplified Bible (AMP)

7 But [even] the very hairs of your head are all numbered. Do not be struck with fear or seized with alarm; you are of greater worth than many [flocks] of sparrows.

Luke 12:24 Amplified Bible (AMP)

24 Observe and consider the ravens; for they neither sow nor reap, they have neither storehouse nor barn; and [yet] God feeds them. Of how much more worth are you than the birds!

After receiving my dual diagnosis and starting treatment I was not able to readily return to school during the second half of the school year in 1989. Many of my classmates had successfully taken their college examinations and started to receive acceptance letters to colleges and universities. Prior to becoming ill with two incurable diseases, I really didn't think about pursuing higher education. My ultimate goal was to graduate from high school.

You see, my mother never encouraged me to go to college; however, she did have high expectations for me to graduate from high school. I attended the same high school my mother did. Graduating from high school would break a generational curse. My mother completed the 11th grade and did not finish high school. She married young and started a family. She could only see where her dreams were deferred and she wanted me to complete her dream of matriculating through high school.

I remember lying on the sofa during the school day surrounded by quietness and the curtains being drawn to keep the sunlight at bay. The sunlight rays of hope had become an enemy to my eyes and depression had made her stay. The sight of sunlight automatically shut my eyelids diminishing any hope of a brighter tomorrow. My body was in excruciating pain and my joints, especially my hands, would lock up on me. My breathing was labored somewhat because my lungs were impacted and I was extremely fatigued.

As my soul looked through the crusted windows of my eyes, I saw wiggle lines known as *floaters* racing back and forth, up and down. I reflected on the detrimental prognosis of my ophthalmologist. He projected that I would be blind by the time I turned 30 years old. Treatment and research for Uveitis was limited, and my future, from his perspective, was not promising. The ophthalmologist also recommended that I begin learning Braille. The eye disease was very aggressive. I had inflammation in all three parts of the eye (uvea).

Actively reflecting on my situation resulted in fear, anxiety and panic, but it also pushed me to pray, prepare and to become proactive in the outcome of my future. I decided that if I went blind I wanted to be an educated woman. Therefore, when I returned to school, I took the SAT. I knew I had to attend a college in the city of Columbia because I had to stay close to medical care and my treatment team. Intercity college application deadlines had expired except for Benedict College (HBCU) because the institution had rolling admission; therefore I applied. I not only applied to college, I applied the Word of God to my life, Philippians 4:13, "I can do all things through Christ which strengthens me."

I graduated from C. A. Johnson High School successfully in 1989.

CHAPTER FOUR

Standing in The Mirror

My body began to change suddenly from the immunosuppressant therapy. I developed a moon face and my body below my neck did not measure up to my face. I looked like a walking lollipop stick. One Sunday at church one of my childhood friends, M. Jackson, recognized the distinct characteristics of my moon face, full and round appearing to almost burst. She approached me after service. I was her mirror, reflecting back Cushing syndrome, a side effect from immunosuppressant therapy. She pulled me to the side and asked, "Are you sick?"

I asked her how she discerned I was sick; she said, "The moon face gave it away." M. Jackson disclosed that she had Lupus. I told her prior to diagnosis it was hypothesized that I could have Lupus because my symptoms were similar to the disease. We had so much in common. She reached out to me, gave me her telephone number, and suggested that we stay connected. M. Jackson was about 5 years my senior. She was more like a big sister. God had sent me a companion, a friend, a confidant and a mentor. She was someone I could pray with, share experiences and face with grace our illnesses together.

2 Corinthians 12:9-11 (NIV) – *But he said to me, "My grace is sufficient for you, for my power is made perfect in weakness." Therefore, I will boast all the more gladly about my weaknesses, so that Christ's power may rest on me. That is why, for Christ's sake, I delight in weaknesses, in insults, in hardships, in persecutions, in difficulties. For when I am weak, then I am strong.*

M. Jackson invited me to attend the Lupus Foundation Support group meetings because there were no support groups for Sarcoidosis in the city or state. Attending the support group provided me with an opportunity to find my voice and fellowship with other women. I remember the first meeting that I attended. I met a rainbow of wonderful, courageous women from all walks of life and ethnic backgrounds. I realized I was not alone in my struggle with accepting my disease and the drastic changes in my body. These women, along with my personal coach, M. Jackson, made me feel like I could take on the world and that it was okay if I had a bad day.

M. Jackson began to have many bad days. She was going in and out of the hospital. Her Lupus had become systematic, and she was becoming weaker in her body but not in her faith in God. M. Jackson soon lost her battle to Lupus, but God gave her the victory over death. She planted many seeds and watered the souls of many through her testimony and the life she lived. As a result, God has given the increase in the lives of those she touched. The most precious lesson M. Jackson taught me is God has given me enough grace to bare my infirmities; therefore, I'm not limited in what I can accomplish because Christ works within me.

I Corinthians 15:10 –*"But by the grace of God I am what I am: and his grace which was bestowed upon me was not in vain; but I labored more abundantly than they all: yet not I, but the grace of God which was with me."*

CHAPTER FIVE
"I Questioned That Love" – *Part 1*

I "Questioned that Love" is a mandated statement my mother would make to me to challenge me to think about my domestic abusive relationship with my first (and only) husband whom I divorced in 1994. Her statement not only challenged me to question my marriage but also my relationship with myself.

My paradigm of myself was distorted. Rejected by my mother on an emotional level due to mental illness and my being conceived as a result of date rape. My biological father abandoned me, and now my body was rejecting me too. My body, my temple that I am to present to God as a living sacrifice, that carried my wounded soul had turned against me. I was becoming angry with God. I was entering into a prison encased with walls of fear, loneliness and abandonment. I was breathing the air of rejection every day. My relationship with myself was almost non-existent. I couldn't accept me or love me because I wasn't taught how to love myself. The spirit of rejection had me bound from the time of my birth. I was conceived in violence, raised in violence, and then I married into violence.

I could not focus on loving me because my view of my future was off focus. I could not see naturally or spiritually that my hurt and pain was working together for my good. I was in a place of despair and desperately needed to feel connected and validated by the human spirit.

Without warning, what appeared to be my knight in shining armor pursued me. A beautiful, physically strong, and caring young man named Jeffery. This beautiful creature made in the image and likeness of God became my focal point. Jeffery became my morning star. He filled my world with joy for a season.

Jeffery became my lighthouse in my dim world of depression, loneliness and abandonment. Jeffery, three years my senior, was my first boyfriend, lover and husband. He was the first man to get my attention and affection at the tender age of 19. I loved him more because he noticed me in the storm of life.

Through God's grace I attended college, with a measure of success. I was listed and honored every semester for being on the Dean's List at Benedict College. I resigned from my job at Family Dollar because I needed to make more money to care for my mother, young brother and myself. I got a new part-time job working at the Baptist Hospital in environmental services. Baptist Hospital is where I met Jeffery the man who would forever have an impact on my life.

Juggling college courses full-time, my part-time job, my family life, and managing my disease was overwhelming. I had no close friends; my depression and low self-esteem were getting the best of me. I had a hard time accepting the changes in my body from the immunosuppressant therapy. I had become preoccupied with my body image. I avoided social situations because I viewed myself as "ugly", and I didn't know who I could be vulnerable with to share my daily struggles.

Jeffery was a force to be reckoned with. He was determined to make himself available to me and become part of my world. Jeffery was nice on the eyes; a handsome young man who could have any woman of his choosing. He pursued me relentlessly, and I rebuffed him at every opportunity. Jeffery noticed me waiting in front of the hospital at night for a cab every evening after 11:00pm to take me home. He waited with me and offered to give me a ride on many occasions and without hesitation I told him "no thank you." Eventually, his big gorgeous smile, charm, and concern about my safety softened my stance and I obliged him and accepted a ride home from him.

Before I knew it, Jeffery was giving me a ride to my doctor's appointments, praying with me, holding my hand, and becoming a supportive friend. Our friendship grew and we both began to share our deepest childhood pains and fears about our futures. We were bonding around our emotional pain and falling quickly in love. I cared so much for Jeffery that I begin to witness to him about Jesus Christ, God's salvation plan for mankind, and God's gift of the Holy Spirit with the evidence of speaking in tongues.

Jeffery started attending church with me. Then one glorious Sunday morning Jeffery was moved with repentance recognizing his sinful nature. When the altar call was made, he made his way to the altar and received Jesus Christ as his Lord and Savior. He was baptized that Sunday night in Jesus' name. He went to tarry service on a Monday night and sought the LORD by calling on His name with a sincere heart. The presence of the LORD overtook him and He received the precious gift of the Holy Spirit with the evidence of speaking with other tongues. The Mothers of the church had given an eyewitness account of this heavenly encounter of him receiving the Holy Spirit.

We were becoming two of a kind, alike in shared life experiences and walking together in faith. We were intertwined, spending all our free time together reading the Word of God, going to church, working, and going to my doctor's appointments. We were becoming one and Jeffery was developing eyes only for me.

Me!!! The girl with an incurable disease whose ophthalmologist predicted that she would lose her eyesight by the time she reached her 30th birthday. Jeffery accepted me and loved me. He proposed to me in 1991, my sophomore year in college. I wasn't ready just yet for marriage because I hadn't earned my college degree. My graduation date was slated for May 1993. I agreed to accept his marriage proposal with the agreement that we will have our nuptials after I graduated from college. We both agreed to a two year engagement.

We were a young couple in waiting. Waiting, waiting, and waiting and spending way too much time together with no one to give an account to. In our waiting to get married we had become husband and wife in our minds. Our waiting gave way to our sexual desires to fully consummate the relationship in the bedroom. The Bible says the marriage bed is undefiled; but we had defiled our bodies and the marriage bed. From our forbidden bedroom encounters I had become full with child.

I was five weeks pregnant when we went to my pediatrician to take a pregnancy test to confirm what my body had already accepted. The nursing staff was very familiar with me because of my frequent follow-up doctor visits. There was contention in the air as we waited for the results. The pregnancy test result was "positive", but it did not bring a positive reaction from the medical staff. Immediately, I was taken into consultation to have an abortion. Yes, an abortion to rid myself of my baby due to potential medical complications and birth defects to the unborn fetus. Keeping the baby could be detrimental to my health and continuation of medical treatment. There was not sufficient medical research on pregnant women taking immunosuppressant drugs and Sarcoidosis.

However, the medical information was not favorable for me to continue treatment. The preferable choice from my treatment team after careful review of medical case studies was for me to have an abortion. I was scared. I had an incurable disease and I was with child. I had no medical road map for what my potential outcomes would be; however, I made a firm decision to keep my baby. There was a small glimmer of hope. The research indicated that during pregnancy women increase steroidal hormones, which could be beneficial to me and serve as an antidote for treatment.

Facing a world of unknown variables, one thing that was certain, Jeffery and I were having a baby. We had to take responsibility for our actions. So, we decided in our own wisdom, to expedite our marriage. We got married on Mother's Day, May 12, 1991 on a Sunday evening. Getting married on Mother's Day was symbolic. It was my gift to my mother because I did not want to bring any shame to her or my family because of my sexual discretions.

My Bishop performed the marital ceremony in his office just before Sunday night service. After praise and worship Bishop brought us before the church and announced us as husband and wife and disclosed that we were with child. What we tried to cover up, our premarital sex was disclosed to the congregation. It was a very awkward moment that I will never forget. It was a celebratory and condemning occasion climaxing at the same time.

We received lots of heartfelt hugs, kisses, and congratulations from our brothers and sisters in Christ after church service. As the parking lot cleared, reality was setting in that we were husband and wife and we had nowhere to lay our heads. We were homeless. During the exchange of warm embrace one of my aunties gave us a monetary gift. We used the money to get a hotel room for a couple of nights.

The weight of fornication was lifted and we were relieved of sexual condemnation and for the first time we were able to make love in a bed that was undefiled. It was a sexual freedom that we had never experienced before. The love-making was beautiful and we were becoming one flesh. For two nights we had a roof over our heads; but check-out time had come and our escapism into paradise had ended. It was time to check-out of the hotel.

As we walked towards the car in the hotel parking lot we were full of fear and anxiety. We faced an unknown road ahead of us because we had no plan. As I began to inquire about our living situation, Jeffery became full of frustration. My conversation was halted due to the stars in my view and the ground coming at me. He punched me in the face! I was in a state of shock, paralyzed, speechless and horrified. The man I loved, became one flesh with, and trusted had physically harmed me. This marked the beginning of the cycle of abuse.

As the marriage progressed we found ourselves in a cycle of homelessness, unemployment and abuse. The abuse at the hands of my husband, Jeffery, expanded from physical abuse to economical, emotional, verbal and mental. He made sure that I understood that he owned me and my human right only came through his authorization. He told me I would never go back to school or work. My role was to serve him, stay at home and raise our children.

As my pregnancy evolved, the stress mounted in the household. Jeffery embarked on having extramarital affairs and the violence intensified as the bills multiplied. I walked on cracking ice everyday not knowing when I was going to slip and say the wrong thing to him that would cause an explosive reaction. Not knowing I had provoked him resulted in his mishandling of me, which caused me to go into premature labor. After the physical altercation, I had severe abdominal pain and strong contractions. Making my way to the bathroom I expelled a bloody substance into the toilet. I bent over the toilet full of pain I was afraid I was going to lose my unborn child.

Frantically, Jeffery rushed me to the emergency room. Upon our arrival to the emergency room without hesitation from the triage unit, I was rushed right to the back to be evaluated and treated. It was discovered via ultrasound that I was having fraternal twins at the emergency room. I had discharged the unborn fetus at home in the toilet.

My contractions had not subsided and the nurse told me I ran the chance of losing the second child if I didn't calm down. She had Jeffery leave the room and asked me a barrage of questions. The most salient question asked was about domestic violence. I felt like a deer caught in headlights. The nurse's question had peeked into my carefully disguised secret that I held in the dark volatile world of exclusion that Jeffery had created for me. I denied the abuse.

Upon Jeffery's return to the treatment room he profusely asked for forgiveness for his physical actions towards me and he kneeled down beside my hospital bed. We prayed for the life of our second child to survive the traumatic event it suffered at the hands of its father. My contractions eased up and came to a halt. I was released from the emergency room to return home with my womb half-full of life and feeling empty at the same time.

Jeffery was becoming docile after the traumatic event of losing one of our unborn children. He appeared to be remorseful and wanted to be held accountable. He sought out our pastor for confession. He told our pastor bluntly, "Yes, I hit my wife and I need prayer." The pastor counseled from:

Ephesians 5:22-33 (NIV) - *22 Wives, submit yourselves to your own husbands as you do to the Lord.23 For the husband is the head of the wife as Christ is the head of the church, his body, of which he is the Savior.24 Now as the* church submits to Christ, so also wives should submit to their husbands in everything.

[25] Husbands, love your wives, just as Christ loved the church and gave himself up for her[26] to make her holy, cleansing[a] her by the washing with water through the word,[27] and to present her to himself as a radiant church, without stain or wrinkle or any other blemish, but holy and blameless.[28] In this same way, husbands ought to love their wives as their own bodies. He who loves his wife loves himself.[29] After all, no one ever hated their own body, but they feed and care for their body, just as Christ does the church—[30] for we are members of his body.[31] "For this reason a man will leave his father and mother and be united to his wife, and the two will become one flesh."[b] [32] This is a profound mystery—but I am talking about Christ and the church.[33] However, each one of you also must love his wife as he loves himself, and the wife must respect her husband.

Our pastor prayed for us and scheduled a few marital counseling sessions to support the marriage. Peace for a season visited our household. Jeffery was blessed with stable employment with SLED as a security guard, we received a housing voucher from the State Housing Authority and I was able to nurture our baby to full term

CHAPTER SIX

"*I Questioned That Love*" – *Part 2*

For 42 weeks I received no treatment for Sarcoidosis and I had no complications. I successfully carried our baby to full term plus two week. Our beautiful baby girl, Hadassah Vashti Fleming, was born via C-section on Christmas Eve December 24, 1991 weighing 8 pounds with no birth defects. To ensure the health of my daughter I was advised by the pediatrician not to breast feed her because of my earlier exposure to immunosuppressant treatment. I was hospitalized for seven days. Prior to my release from the hospital my mother offered me to stay with her as I recovered from the medical procedure and to help me care for her first grandchild. Jeffery agreed to the arrangement because he worked at night and close monitoring was needed.

My mother was a great help to me. My mother birthed my two brothers and myself by C-section. She had experience, firsthand experience, of what a woman's body goes through after giving birth through C-section. I needed my mother and I was glad that she was able to be there for me emotionally as I embarked on this new chapter of motherhood. In the short few weeks at her home, my mother taught me how to hold and care for my newborn.

My intimate and much needed time with my mother at her home ended abruptly. The pressure of fatherhood and added responsibility was getting the best of Jeffery. He came over to my mother's house one evening to drop off diapers and other baby items. We sat on the sofa and very few words were exchanged. The tension he brought into the house could be cut with a knife. I removed myself from the living room and went into the kitchen. I had learned to read the cues of a physical assault coming my way. I wasn't able to alleviate the onslaught on his hands. He came into the kitchen and punched me in the face. His explanation for punching me was that I didn't say thank you for him bringing over the baby supplies. Trust me, I thanked him when he entered my mother's house. I guess he failed to hear me because he was so full of rage.

My nose took most of the impact of his fist making contact with my face. I let out a loud squeal, tried to hold back my tears and hush my outbursts from the pain I had just encountered. Blood was flowing from my nostrils and making contact with my mother's white carpet as I proceeded to get away from his fierce hands. My mother heard the commotion downstairs and unknowingly she was getting ready to learn of our family secret of domestic violence. Mother beheld the bloody scene and got directly in Jeffery's personal space. What have you done to my daughter? My mother was in disbelief and was literally about to go into attack mode to protect me, her only daughter. Jeffery quickly left mother's house.

My mother was shaken up and started shouting at me "I questioned that love." What man hits his wife after she has given birth to their child? After having a C-section, being gutted like a pig and so close to death. "I questioned that love." I did not understand what she said to me at that time. My mother called the police and the paramedics. The police wrote up the incident and asked me if I wanted to press charges for the assault. I hesitated; however, with persuasion from my mother and the police officers I followed through with pressing charges, resulting in a warrant for his arrest.

I reneged on carrying through with the first warrant to have Jeffery prosecuted for hitting me. I was still in love with the idea of being in love and having a marriage. I wanted to hold on to the dream of having a happy loving family. How could I prosecute the father of my baby? I felt like I was betraying him. I saw him as a victim of life circumstances; I could not see myself. I only saw him. I was being the subservient wife. I left my mother's house and went back home to a place where peace once reigned but was now filled with anxiety all over again.

Throughout these grim times I sought spiritual counseling from my pastor. I informed him that my husband was still aggressive towards me. I wanted my pastor to tell me to leave my husband and take refuge in a safe place. My pastor would listen with discerning ears, give me some consoling words and conclude each session by telling me to go home and pray. I went home to a place where the cycle of financial instability was being executed again along with the physical and emotional abuse. The financial instability wasn't because Jeffery didn't have enough money to pay the household bills. He purposely misallocated the money towards his own pleasures and rendezvous. He was living out life as a single man in spite of his official title "married man."

As the pages of my life continued to turn from nightmare to nightmare I conceived our second child. Jeffery's fiscal responsibility had become so negligent that my mother and my family were becoming more aware of the deplorable living conditions. The utility bills were not paid resulting in the lights and water being turned off frequently. Food and diapers were scarce. I had no other choice but to reach out to my mother. My mother provided me with food and formula, and she purchased cloth diapers. She taught me how to put the cloth diapers on my baby and how to clean them in a bucket. When I would go to my mother's house for supplies she would look me directly in the eyes and say, "I questioned that love."

The poor living environment in our home didn't bother Jeffery because he worked two jobs and was barely in the house. And he knew that if things got too unbearable I could return to my mother's house. However, my mother was getting tired of the back and forth routine from my house to her house. In fact, my entire family was getting tired of my unending cycle of abuse that had somehow enlisted them. Open doors to help me escape the abusive hands of my husband were closing. As the doors were closing my prayer life was opening wide to accommodate my prayer requests to meet my daily needs, especially my sanity.

Psalm 37:5 – *I was young and now I am old, yet I have never seen the righteous forsaken or their children begging bread.*

Isaiah 26:3 – *You will keep in perfect peace those whose minds are steadfast, because they trust in you.*

Jeffery's physical attacks and explosive outbursts were becoming infrequent; however, they had intensified. I was getting strong but I had not yet discovered my strength. I gleaned my potential strength to flee the hands of my husband when he put the lives of my daughter, unborn child, and me on a chaotic drive down Two Notch Road. We were heading to Columbia Mall and our conversation turned into him having a verbal and physical altercation with me while driving. He threatened to kill all of us, with one hand on the steering wheel and his other hand punching me as the car was bearing toward the guard rails on the highway at a speed over 90 miles per hour. This was the closest I ever came to death at my husband's hands.

All, I could say was "JESUS!" My life was flashing in front of me. I begged him to stop and slow the car down and to think about our daughter's life. He snapped out of his destructive trance, but he was still in a hypnotic state. He pulled the car over into the mall parking lot. I jumped out of the car rescued my daughter from the back seat from the baby car seat and ran into the mall to escape him and to find safety. I went up to the first security officer and quickly asked for the police.

I was most concerned for the life of our daughter and my unborn child in my womb. Caring for my infant daughter and pregnant with my second child, I was compelled to protect my children. I spoke with the police without hesitation. I agreed to proceed with a warrant for Jeffery's arrest. The warrant was issued and Jeffery and I had a court date. I lived between my mother's house and my house as I waited for the court date to arrive. The appointed court date had come. We were standing before the judge and as the judge read the charges filed against Jeffery, I realized I wanted the hands of justice to punish my husband for all the times he hit me. I wanted the hands of justice to hold him accountable. Perhaps, the halls of justice would bring about a change in his behavior.

Standing before the judge as if they were friends, Jeffery did not deny the charges. Much to my surprise the judge only gave Jeffery a harsh warning. I paraphrase the judge's warning: "I'm going to be lenient with you because you work for SLED (police agency), and I will let you off with a warning. However, if you come back to this court house for abusing your wife, I'm going to put you so far under the jailhouse I won't know when is the next time you will see sunlight." The judge dismissed the charges. My voice and my petition were negated. The scales of justice had failed me, and the hands of my church had failed me too. All I wanted was someone to advocate for me, to speak truth to power. I wanted my pastor to tell me to leave my husband, and I wanted the justice system to make him accountable for his actions of violence against our children and me. It was crystal clear to me that the good old boys' network had Jeffery's best interest in mind ensuring that he maintained control over his household and dominion over me.

Jeffery continued with his sporadic behavior of highs and lows emotionally and physically with me. With each blow I was getting stronger and my prayer life was increasing. I heard the LORD loud and clear one evening when my husband came home from work. I was standing in the living room holding our 8 month old daughter when he entered the house. Hadassah clung close to me when she saw him and heard his voice. As he reached for her, she flinched and clung even closer to me. He snatched his daughter out of my arms and said no child of mine is going to refuse to come to me. With his huge hands he clinch her and she begin to cry intensely out of fear. Jeffery became enraged because his baby girl did not want him to hold her. He felt rejected. As a result he took his big massive hand and spanked her on her thighs.

My eyes couldn't believe what I was seeing. My daughter's father was hitting her thighs repeatedly. I tried with all my might to retrieve my daughter from her father's arms. Each time I tried to release my baby girl from her father's arms he pushed me to the carpet. The question that I pondered in the dark places of my mind: Would my husband abuse my children? And the answer was a resounding "YES." The legacy of abuse would include my children too. Jeffery hit our daughter 8 times on her pimply thighs. She cried and he held her close and wouldn't let her go.

I was in disbelief of what had just happened. I went into our bedroom and I began to cry and pray. I was planting seeds of hope with every tear drop that I cried. I prayed fervently, I prayed, "LORD, please change my husband." I mourned, I begged God, "LORD please change my husband." I saw our future: An abusive marriage possibly ending in death, my daughter growing up believing its normal for men to abuse women, and a son who would be indoctrinated to believe he is justified to beat a female. I prayed even harder with every tear, "LORD please change my husband." Then, there was quietness all around me. I felt the presence of the almighty God!

God anointed my ears and he began to speak to me. "If you have faith the size of a mustard seed you can move a mountain. I can't change your husband's heart to stop abusing his family because he doesn't want to change. I have given every man a free will and I will not force your husband to change. If he has faith the size of mustard seed then I can minister unto him but he has no faith that he can change his violent sin nature." I had a light bulb moment in prayer. It was like an epiphany, a change had come over me. The presence of God was all over me and I broke out in uncontrollable laughter. I rolled around on the floor laughing with God. A change was coming.

By this time, I had left Jeffery all together 9 times and my mother was growing tired of the merry-go-round scenario. Apprehension was building in her home because there was no normalcy of residence with me. My mother's neighbors and apartment manager had taken notice of my unstable living arrangements. I was not on my mother's lease and this could pose a potential problem for my mother's housing. I returned to my desolated home and continued to find comfort in prayer. I was nearing the end of my second pregnancy. The year 1992 was coming to an end and Hadassah was turning 1 year old. Jeffery was still having extra martial affairs and he was barely home. It was Christmas Eve and Hadassah's birthday. During the day I came across a department store catalogue while cleaning and I thumbed through the pages where Jeffery had highlighted various items including jewelry. There was nothing highlighted in the catalogue that would be useful for our daughter, our unborn son, or me. When my husband came home from work and I asked him about the catalogue and the items highlighted and the jewelry, without hesitation he told me the items were for his lover not me.

He came home with nothing in his hands to celebrate neither our daughter's first birthday nor a gift for Christmas. I admonished him for forgetting about his daughter's birthday. He went to the Wal-Mart and purchased her a baby walk-and-ride pushcart and a he got a can opener for me. Little did he know the baby walk-and-ride cart and can opener were symbols that I was getting ready to walk-and-ride through the open doors of opportunities for a better life for my daughter and my unborn son.

The Wal-Mart incident became an epic event pushing me into survival mode. We went toWal-Mart to purchase diapers for our son who was about two months old. Jeffery told me to stay in the car and wait for his return from the store. For some reason, I did not listen. After he exited the car I waited for him to get several feet away from the car, then I got out with our children. As I was approaching the entrance to the store, I noticed Jeffery talking to two females in a friendly and intimate manner inside the sliding doors. I slowed down my pace to observe their interactions.

Jeffery moved farther into the store to get what he had come to purchase. Once I had made it into the front entrance of the store there was a fast food station. I decided not to advance beyond this point. As I waited for Jeffery, the same two ladies that he had conversed with came towards me and started looking over my baby boy and making statements about his appearance. I recognized one of them, the lover of my husband, because she had left her imprint on my home when I was not there and she even came to my front door and asked me for my husband. I became outraged and told her to stay away from my husband and my family. I told her I would kill her. I don't know what came over me. For the first time, I was venting my emotions. My numbness had come alive.

Infuriated, I barreled down the store aisles with the shopping cart with the children secured looking for Jeffery in the store. He was amazed to see me as I came charging at him and informing him that I told his lover to stay away from him, my family and I that I would kill her if she didn't. He grabbed me hesitantly, "Didn't I tell you to stay in the car? You didn't listen to me." He kept me very close to him; purchased items at the check-out counter and he did not say another word as we exited the store heading back to the car. The car was absolutely quiet, even the children were quiet. A quiet storm was broiling and I knew I did not want to go home. I asked Jeffery to take me to my mother's house. He agreed to take me. I wanted to get away from him before his fist struck a blow. The storm had come to a peak and his blows came towards me while he was driving the car down Sunset Blvd. With each blow matching every word that came out of his mouth, "Didn't I, tell, you, to, stay, in, the, car." He repeated himself several times and the rounds of blows were repetitious. I tried my best to remain calm and I called on Jesus inside of my head. I wanted his other hand to stay steady on the steering wheel because my children's safety was important to me and I did not want to cause an accident.

My children and I made it in one piece to my mother's house. My visit was unexpected on a Saturday afternoon. I had not visited or stayed at my mother's house for a while. My mother had gotten use to me not coming over with my domestic affairs. Now, here I was again at her doorsteps, knocking on the door this time with two children in my arms, seeking refuge from the mighty fist of my husband. My mother half-heartedly let me come through the revolving doorway into an unwelcoming atmosphere. My mother knew the routine and she was tired of being engrafted into my world of turmoil. She wanted some stability for herself and wanted me to take responsibility for the decisions I made. My mother didn't say too much to me this time. She kept her distance most of the day. As the evening time drew near, she became more aggravated and began to speak to me in a hostile manner regarding my marriage. It was as if she wanted to provoke me to argue with her to the point of leaving her house. She looked me squarely in the face and told me, "If you were a real woman your husband wouldn't cheat on you or hit you." Now she had pushed me to strike back with fighting words. I told her at least all my children are from one man. Within seconds my mother had lunged at me, pushed me up against the wall and began to bang my head up against the wall. It was never my intention to disrespect my mother, but my mouth had no control at this point.

I did not fight my mother back. I was used to being pinned down and receiving blows from hands that are supposed to protect me. Once her fit of rage was over, she jumped into her car and drove to her sister's house. That night I sat on the bed in the room that was once mine and pondered my mother's declarative statement that she had posed to me the first night she became aware of my abuse: "I questioned that love." And I finally had a response to her rhetorical assertions. "Love doesn't hurt."

1 Corinthians 13:4 – *Love is patient, love is kind. It does not envy, it does not boast, it is not proud.*

I bedded the children down for the night in the crib my mother placed in the room. My baby boy wasn't feeling well and he had a high temperature. I monitored him all night as I convinced myself not to return to my husband. I hoped that upon sunrise Sunday morning my mother and I could work out a peaceful solution, where I could buy sometime at her house to figure out an action plan to break the chain of abuse. The plan could not be developed in the place where the beginning of the abuse had begun. My mother returned to the house still with a hostile disposition. My auntie called to check on us, and I informed her that my mother wasn't speaking to me. My mother overheard the conversation. She came out of her bedroom and verbally attacked me for talking about her. My conversation with my auntie had ended and the onslaught of my mother's fire was upon me. I called the police. The police came out to assess the volatile situation and informed me that, for the sake of peace, I needed to leave her home since I didn't live there.

I looked at my two children resting in the dilapidated crib and I prayed, "LORD, help me to love my children and love them beyond the pain and hurt I suffered at the hands of their father. Teach me LORD how to love them and provide for them." As I gazed into their beautiful eyes, immediately my daughter became my hope and my son became my inspiration. I was determined that no one would ever hit me again or have an opportunity to abuse my children. With a few coins in my pocket I left my mother's house and caught the bus downtown. I had nowhere to go, but a determination not to return to an abusive home or marriage. I was now operating in survivor mode. I had to survive.

CHAPTER SEVEN
Guardian Angels

Psalm 91:11 (NIV) – *For he will command his angels concerning you to guard you in all your ways.*

A guardian angel is a person or spiritual being assigned to you by God to care for and watch over you. God provided me with many guardian angels to help me transition from being a victim to a survivor. I was alone downtown on a Sunday afternoon with nowhere to go, with an infant and a toddler. I was vulnerable and in distress. We sat at the bus stop across from the Oliver Gospel Mission; a homeless shelter that I was very familiar with because I walked passed it frequently when I went into the inner city. I always observed the men and women loitering around the building quite harmless to those who passed by. They seemed to be waiting in expectation that someone was available to help them get back on their mission to succeed in life. I needed help. I needed a safe place so I could get off the street with my two children. So, I went across the street to the brick building that appeared to have open arms to receive us. I spoke with the social worker and explained I needed to change my son's diaper; needed water to make a bottle of formula, and my daughter was hungry. The social worker allowed us to stay and rest in the community room and provided us with food to eat.

We had a moment of peace with uncertainty. The sun was setting and the social worker politely told me we had to leave the facility because shelter services would only render to adults not children. With much hesitation it was frightening to accept that we had to leave the open arms that had once received us earlier in the day to only be placed back on the street. As I gathered the baby bag and our jackets, the case manager provided me with directions to the Salvation Army Shelter located a few blocks down the street that accepted women with children. I was told to get to the location before 6:00pm because it was first come first served.

It was dust, nearly dark, and I needed to get to the Salvation Army Shelter before the last bed was taken. I walked as fast as I could down the street with my baby boy strapped in front of me, my daughter on my waist and the diaper bag on my shoulder. I was 'a woman on a mission' to never return to the hands of abuse. I made it to the hotel site that served as the shelter behind the church. I joined the long line of men, women, and a few children from all walks of life in need of refuge for the night. The case manager was paring the clients to share rooms based on gender, family and social norms. I was paired with a rather eccentric looking older woman with a mouth full of profanity who had been there a few nights before. She was muttering underneath her breath about how much she didn't want to share the room with me. And, out of nowhere, a young lady approached the case manager and stated her family had a crib in their room with an extra bed, and it would be best if we stayed with them. I was reassigned to share rooms with the married couple and their child.

As we walked from the parking lot of the premises the young lady began to tell me why she and her husband decided to share their space with me. First, she told me I needed to get out of that purple dress I was wearing because it made me an easy target to being attacked sexually. She sized me up and gave me a pair of her jeans and a t-shirt to put on. Then she told me the roommate assigned to me originally had a mental problem, had a nasty attitude and was argumentative. Simply put, the husband said, "You need to be protected, and we can provide that for you." I felt like I could trust them. I did feel safe.

There was warmness to the couple's presence. We talked and shared why we were seeking shelter. Through our conversation, I learned they had relocated from "The Big Apple," New York City. They asked if I would help them navigate the city because they had never been to South Carolina. So, we worked in partnership. They provided me with protection and I traveled with them in their car serving as a GPS system, directing them to the address of apartments, employment services and the Department of Human Services.

We worked together in agreement from the beginning of the week up until mid-week. We ate breakfast together at the adjacent church. I was up for our new adventure for the day. Traveling around Columbia with my new found friends gave me a sense of freedom and escapism. However, their plans for Wednesday did not include me giving them directions because they had found their way. They had some personal business to take care of and they had become familiar with the highways to finding their way around the city.

I had no plan or nowhere to go after breakfast. All clients had to leave the shelter and could not return until the evening when the doors would open again to serve. We said good-bye for the day and my beloved friends drove off in their car with their tasks for the day. Little did I know this would be my last good bye to them and to Columbia, the city of my birth. Feeling abandoned and all alone, I left the church after breakfast with my children with no plan for that day or the next. I had spent the previous three days helping my friends from New York get established in their new territory of residence. I had invested no time brainstorming or planning my next steps. I knew one thing for sure, I wasn't returning home. Needing a safe place for my children and serenity to think, I headed towards the park behind the Post Office.

As I was crossing the street, a scruffy looking man who appeared to be drunk, started yelling at me from the top of the hotel balcony that oversaw the church, which faced the street I was crossing. He yelled, "Hey you, battered woman." I kept walking; however, at a much faster pace. He yelled again, "Hey you, battered woman." I stopped and looked across the street at him. He said, bluntly, "Yes, I'm talking to you." He yelled, "Go to Center Place, they can help you. You need to go to Center Place." This man did not know me. How did he know my situation and circumstance? Who told him? His appearance got my attention, the commending tone of his voice suggested that I follow his advice. It seemed reasonable to go since I had no agenda for the day. Center Place resonated with me because I had seen the building many times as I traveled on the transit bus into the city.

I walked with my children at least three miles to Center Place. I signed in and waited for my number to be called. I met with the case manager and she did a needs assessment. Becoming aware of my domestic affairs, she inquired if there were any family members or friends that I could stay with to get me off the streets into a more secure environment for my family. I told her my family had helped me as much as they could. She pressed me the more, is there anybody else you can think of? There was someone, but he lived in Washington, D.C., my father Roger. She pondered for a moment. "I feel that it is urgent that I get you and your family off the streets, so I'm going to do something that is not the normal procedure. We have something here called Traveler AID. Traveler AID is a set aside fund used to help stranded people get back home to their state of residence. I'm going to breach the rules for you and provide you with a one-way Greyhound ticket to Washington, D.C. All I need is to verify that your father is willing to receive you."

My father was working down at the shipyard in Southwest D.C., and he could not be reached by phone. The case manager called my step-mother at the FCC, she confirmed kinship, and was readily available to help execute the escape plan to leave South Carolina. A way of escape had been open to me. However, I wasn't sure. Everything was happening so quickly. I had no time to think and I had no plan yet. It seemed as if a getaway plan had been prepared for me in advance. I reflected on the strange man telling me to go to Center Place and yes, he was right, the Center provided me with an escape plan. I accepted the voucher for the one-way ticket to D.C. God had a plan for my life and He assigned guardian angels to provide provision, protection and providence for my children and I.

Jeremiah 29:11 (NIV) – *For I know the plans I have for you," declares the LORD, "plans to prosper you and not to harm you, plans to give you hope and a future.*

CHAPTER EIGHT
The Lord Said "Go"

Genesis 12:1(NIV) – *"The LORD said to Abram, "Go from your country, your people, and your father's household to the land I will show you."*

Luke 4:24 (NIV) – *"Truly I tell you," no prophet is accepted in his hometown. "*

As I held the bus ticket in my hand I realized I had enough of fighting. I had no alternative but to fly into action and seize the opportunity to leave South Carolina, with my two children at the tender age of 22, on a one-way Greyhound ticket to Washington, D.C. I had no money in my pocket, but I had hope and inspiration in my arms and heart. I loved my children and they gave me the courage to believe that we could have a better tomorrow.

Evening had approached and the time had come for us to board the bus. There were no hugs and kisses to see us off. Not making a phone call to my husband and mother was intentional because I knew if I heard their voices they could have persuaded me to stay in a barren situation. I knew they couldn't be a part of my new life until I was able to get myself established and secure. My desire to have their love and approval was detrimental to me starting a "new life." My heart was aching because I had to leave my marriage and mother 478 miles behind. It was only me and a prayer for God's protection as we braved the elements of the unknown. As the bus pulled off, I felt the cut of the umbilical cord of pain and rejection being left behind. As the bus traveled up the highway on 95 North, the chains of domestic abuse were being broken and its links were dropped along the roadside, never to be reconnected again.

Psalm 30:5 – "...*his favor lasts a lifetime; weeping may stay for the night, but rejoicing comes in the morning.*"

The full moon was chasing me on the bus reminding me that after you have mourned for a while joy comes in the morning. It was a quiet bus ride as the children slept peacefully; but I dared not close my eyes. My eyes stayed fixated on the moon. It appeared to be larger than other nights that had previously passed. The moon was so close to the earth. It guided the bus and my dreams down the dark spiraling road. As the bus drove farther into the night, I cried tears of joy and pain; Tears of joy because freedom had availed herself to me; Tears of pain because I was mourning the loss of a marriage that was choked by the hands of self-hate.

The night hours were moving swiftly into morning. The bus had two major layovers in Fayetteville, NC and Richmond, VA with short stops in between state lines. As the bus pushed up the road, I sensed the evaluation in my life that had yet to be manifested. Full of expectation of receiving love from a man I had not known for most of my life. A man I called father because his last name was all I had known for most of my life. I was attached to him by namesake only. A last name I inherited from a marriage he once had with my mother. I did not inherit his genes. However, I inherited his heart.

The bus had arrived to the nation's capital. With his arms open wide my father received my children and I in the bus terminal. My father's arms embraced me, and with a warm salutation he stated, "Welcome to DC."

CHAPTER NINE
Pursuing Hope and Inspiration

Hope is a feeling of optimism or a desire that something will happen.

Jeremiah 29:11 - *¹¹"For I know the plans I have for you," declares the LORD, "plans to prosper you and not to harm you, plans to give you hope and a future." (NIV)*

Inspiration is something that makes someone want to do something or that gives someone an idea about what to do or create.

John 16:13 - *¹³"But when he, the Spirit of truth, comes, he will guide you into all the truth. He will not speak on his own; he will speak only what he hears, and he will tell you what is yet to come."*

Washington, D.C. became my Canaan land, a strange land full of forbidden fruit, giants, and open doors of opportunities. I secured my first apartment in Carver Terrance located in the ghetto in the NE corridor of Washington D.C. in Ward 7 known for its prostitution, frequent murders and drug trafficking. My father worked for the real estate company that owned the apartment building; he was able to get my rent reduced to coincide with my monthly welfare check.

My residential environment could have discouraged me and caused me to lose my hope and give up my inspiration. The apartment complex was quiet by day, like a sleeping giant. However, as the sun retired for the day the courtyards became a social scene. The residents and patrons partook in their nightly activities of alcohol drinking, drugging, fighting and sexing. The laughter of children playing and crying rung out during the night hours until day break as their guardians engaged in their demoralizing behaviors. I observed all of this from my apartment window.

I prayed for the Lord to protect my children and I. I remembered something that one of the ministers at my home church in SC said one Sunday night; the minister said, "It's going to come a time in your life when you are going to need the Word of God and there is going to be famine in the land. So, store up the Word of God and hide it in your heart so when the time comes you will have the word in you to sustain you."

Numbers 13:28-33 – *28 "But the people who live there are powerful, and the cities are fortified and very large. We even saw descendants of Anak there. 29 The Amalekites live in the Negev; the Hittites, Jebusites and Amorites live in the hill country; and the Canaanites live near the sea and along the Jordan." 30Then Caleb silenced the people before Moses and said, "We should go up and take possession of the land, for we can certainly do it."...33 ... We seemed like grasshoppers in our own eyes, and we looked the same to them."*

I was living among giants. I was like a grasshopper, fragile yet maintaining my composure because I put my trust in the LORD. Several months had passed and I was feeling at ease in my hostile environment. I realized that I had become part of the community. The boys in the hood looked out for me. For example, when I caught a ride home with the courtesy driver to transport my grocery from the Safeway, one of the thugs loitering out front of my apartment building would help me bring my groceries up the long stair case to the fourth floor to my apartment door never making an attempt to enter in. The thugs respected me and never tried to make any sexual advances towards me either. The older women in the building would sit in their windows and kept an eye on my comings and goings. I was beginning to feel a hedge of protection surrounding my family and I.

One summer morning, I took my children out to play on the front steps outside our apartment building. The sun was shining bright. The matriarch of the building, Mrs. Pearlean, an elderly lady who was graced with salt & pepper hair well seasoned in wisdom joined us. She began to inquire about who I was and where I was from. I told her Columbia, South Carolina. With excitement in her eyes and voice she exclaimed, "I have a family member who attended Benedict College in Columbia." What a coincidence. I informed her that I attended Benedict College. She asked me if I knew her relative because we attended college during the same time period. I told her I'm not good with names; better with faces. I asked her to watch my kids play as I went back to my apartment to retrieve my college yearbooks.

We perused the college yearbooks together. My desire to go back to college grew as the pages turned and I blurted out, "I wish I could go back to school." Mrs. Pearlean, spoke as if she was my Fairy Godmother, "you can go back to college and finish your degree." But how was I going to do that with no money and childcare?

Philippians 4:19 (NIV) – *"And my God will meet all your needs according to the riches of his glory in Christ Jesus."*

Mrs. Pearlean informed me that there is a university in the city that I can afford, the University of the District of Columbia. She advised me to speak with my social worker and inquire about their welfare to work program. Stepping out on faith, I started attending the University of the District of Columbia (UDC) in August 1993, the same year I arrived to D.C. Me, a single mother of two small children, an infant and a 1 year old, walked through the open door of higher education to finish my college degree.

CHAPTER TEN

Opening Pandora's Box

Every time I placed my key into the lock of my door to my first apartment it was euphoric. Walking across the threshold of the doorway was exhilarating knowing I wouldn't have to anticipate or nervously await the hands of abuse to touch me. The small one-bedroom apartment provided me space to exhale and relax my body from years of being on hyper alert.

I had a routine that I followed upon returning home from my long extended day at college. I would prepare dinner for the children, then have play time to ensure a quiet night so I could study. Lastly, I would give them a nice warm bath. My babies were usually in the bed before 8:00pm.

Then it was my time. I would turn out the lights, have a bath, burn my candles and incense, turn on some smooth jazz, journal and do my homework, once I had placed my children to bed. I was more than content. I was coming into my womanhood. I could hear my voice; because there was only one voice in the room. In those quite moments of self-reflection, I realize I was standing on my own two feet. I was optimistic about my future. I filed for a divorce.

My weekday school schedule started at 6:00am in the morning. With punctuality I got the children up and ready to go to daycare and gathered all of my textbooks and materials for all my classes to ensure we had everything we needed for the day. I meticulously coordinated the metro bus schedules to arrive to school on time. I took three different metro buses to get to UDC and my return each day. My school day was from 8:00am to 4:00pm. Going to school was my full-time job. Juggling my responsibilities as a mother and going to school full-time was a challenging task. However, I was focused and determined to complete my bachelor's degree.

The demands of completing course work assignments, single parenting, and no family support were taking a toll on me. Coming home daily to an apartment that had only one voice, which was mine, was conducive for me to have a mental breakdown. I recall my child psychology professor saying, "Single parenting is abnormal behavior." Her thought-provoking hypothesis created a heated discussion among my colleagues with me leading the debate that single parenting is not abnormal. Sometime later, I realized her profound statement was true. The demands placed on a single parent were not designed for one parent but two parents. Therefore, a supportive community is needed if the single-family unit is to balance its psychological demands. My divorce was granted on September 15, 1994.

My immediate family was in South Carolina. I had protective walls up towards my children's father and my mother. These protective walls were within normalcy considering the emotional and psychological abuse I had endured. My father was unable to avail himself to me like he wanted to due to blended family issues.

Coping with the demands of my life, anger, resentment, and bitterness gently gave way to the Pandora's Box opening slowly but surely. I continued in the same pattern year after year while matriculating through undergraduate school. Depression, anger, and fear began to creep in and invade my apartment and my mind. The flashback of childhood memories within the crevasses of my mind had come to the front of my mind.

This only amounted to daily stress given rise to the Sarcoidosis and uveitis becoming aggressively active again. Frequent medical doctor visits were now included in my already vigorous daily routine. From 1991 to 1994 I was asymptomatic. I had gone years with no treatment for the disease.

The uveitis was impacting both of my eyes in the front and the back. A new treatment modality was introduced to control the inflammation at the back of my eyes. My treatment regimen consisted of steroidal anti-inflammatory medications: eye drops, pills and needle injections into my eyes. Yes, injections into my eyes. The needle extended from the front of the eye to the back of the eye. The injection into my eye felt like an icy piercing. I could not oppose the eye injections because there was no alternative treatment.

The pressures of trying to maintain equilibrium were surrounding me. I had taken my eyes off of God. My eyes could only fixate on the gods of my past: anger, fear, and unforgiveness. I felt like God had turned His back on me. I felt disconnected from God. I had become angry with Him. I could not understand at the time why God would allow so much persecution in my life. Not realizing the good, bad, and ugly was working for my good. I was an angry woman who had turned her eyes away from God, but I never stopped praying.

In spite of my endless bouts of sickness, single parenting, depression and loneliness, I graduated from the University of the District of Columbia in 1996 with my Bachelors of Arts Degree in Psychology. I completed my course work in three years. In the fall of the same year that I graduated, I started my graduate studies at Trinity University.

Within months of completing my undergraduate degree, my welfare caseworker informed me that I needed to find a job because their program is not designed to help women with college degrees. All my government benefits were slated to stop in August of 1996. Frantically, I begin to search for a job and became gainfully employed working as a bank teller for Crestar Bank. This was the beginning of my working resume. From 1993 to 1996 I did not work. Obtaining my bachelor's degree was my full-time job.

I was now working full-time, raising a family, chronically ill, and attending graduate school. I was on "overload." By this time I was immersed in my graduate course work I was near a nervous breakdown and I was legally blind in my right eye due to cataracts.

The pressures of life's circumstance had opened the Pandora's Box wide open. My inner conflicts were now out of the once secured box and refused to shut up. I was awakened early in the morning on February 12, 1998. I could not sleep because my thought patterns were in an embryonic stanza as I wrote this letter to my mother:

Dear Mom:

Mom, where are you? I have been trying to find you for quite some time. Right now it's 3:00am in the morning and I cannot sleep. I had a dream about you and you were hitting me in the face. I remember you hitting me in the face. I remember the times that you pinned me down to the floor and attacked me. I remember never receiving love from the vessel that created me.

Mom, where are you? I never got to know you. You are a figment of my imagination. You are a silhouette in the midst of my night.

I know that you were there, but what I don't know is a mother's love. I wanted you to touch me and protect me. I wanted you to caress me and hold me so tight that I could feel your life force being radiated all over me. An exchange of energy between you and me would have created our intimacy. Yes, today I still crave a mother's love.

I have searched for that love in many places. The search has led me to many valleys and graves within the dark places of my mind and on this earth. I have searched for it in material things, and relationships never seemly to find the sweet treasures of a mother's love. There is a void, that runs so deep within my soul and it can only be filled by a mother's love.

Love,

Your Daughter,
Bridget

At the time that I penned this letter, I never intended to give the letter to my mother. I just needed to get the images and thoughts out of my head. My mind was a flutter with bits and pieces of my abusive my past. It was like a jigsaw puzzle. I was also having flashbacks as if the physical and sexual abuse was taking place in my now moment. I remember a promise that I made to myself; "I will never have a nervous breakdown. Before I do I would check myself into the hospital." I watched my mother have several nervous breakdowns and each time it took her longer to bounce back. I had to think of my children. What would happen to them if I had a mental breakdown? A breakdown was not an option for me because there would be no one to pick up the pieces. I had to be strong and maintain my mental health.

I checked myself into Howard University Hospital because I was mentally and emotional exhausted. My hospitalization did not interfere with my graduate studies because I had ended the spring semester successfully. I was in a position to get the help I needed. I was hospitalized for several days on the 5th floor of the psychiatric unit.

Journal Entry: May 11, 1998

I'm currently in Howard University Hospital on the psychiatric floor. I can't believe that I'm here. I feel like I'm my mother. I would have never thought that I would be here. However, I'm here.

I'm also afraid because I do not know the outcome of the process. I know that I have emotional problems and I'm afraid that they wouldn't be solved. I have been working hard for the past two years in individual and group therapy. I know that I have accomplished a lot in those sessions. I feel that I should feel better now and be much happier. However, I'm not. I think I'm angry more now because I have released so many painful memories.

The memories and thoughts play in my head; not one thought or memory but many. My racing thoughts are all negative. What do I want out of this process?

I want a new beginning. I want to wake up in the morning with happiness. I want a zeal for life. I want to feel life. I want to see God again in all His creations. I want to feel the energy of the universe. I want God to breathe on me. I want to live again. I want to wake up from this nightmare. I want to be free!!!

Journal Entry: May 12, 1998

Acceptance is the process of living; being able to embrace your past and future. Accepting the fact that you are an agent of change; and change is a process of acceptance.
God, I want to change because "change is good." I want to be the best that I can be. I want to set a great example for my children. I must be an agent of change because I hold my children's future in my hand.

I must not be afraid. I must not be in denial. I must accept that I have a condition known as depression. Depression is part of who I am. However, it doesn't control my destiny. I create my future because I am an agent of change. Let the chain reaction begin.

Journal Entry: May 13, 1998

Right now I'm afraid. I want to change. I want to let my past go. I want to beat this depression. It's like I'm afraid to live for now. I'm afraid to move forward. I want a better life. I remember the Bible, says "joy comes in the morning." Many mornings have come and I was unable to bring joy to it. I look forward to the day I can bring joy to my mornings.

Journal Entry: May 14, 1998

I've been at the bottom of the valley trying to pull myself out. When I look up I see the light. I want to feel the light shine all over me; the rays of sunlight beaming upon my face; Embracing and bathing me with all of its glory. I want to feel the sun again. I want its energy to vibrate and enrich my soul. I want to make love to the sun and become one with it for eternity.

Journal Entry: May 15, 1998

I did not sleep well last night. My roommate talks in her sleep. However, my goal for today is to think positively. I realize that I have control over my life. I determine my destiny. I create with the words that I speak. Words are powerful for they direct my path in life. Therefore, choose positive words to express your destiny.

Journal Entry: May 16, 1998

Today, I feel great. My head feels very clear. I think the medicine is working. I was diagnosed with dysthymia/depression. Once discharged from the hospital, I continued psychotherapy to better manage my life and confront the demons of my past. Getting the mental help that I needed enabled me to see my way again. The path God predestined for me from the beginning of time was becoming clear.

I received my Masters of Arts, in Community Health Promotion and Education, from Trinity University in 1999. In spite of my trials and tribulations in six years, I successfully earned two degrees with God's grace.

CHAPTER ELEVEN
God Gave Sight To The Blind

From 1995 to 1999 my vision was deteriorating fast. The inflammation in both eyes was out of control and no course of treatment was working. The bleak reality of blindness was approaching me. My eye doctor had come to the conclusion that he had no other treatment options for me. The fear of blindness put me in a dark place of despair. However, there was a glimmer of hope. My doctor referred me to the National Eye Institute located on the campus of the National Institute of Health in Bethesda, Maryland. I was enrolled in a clinical trial.

Mark 8:22-25 – *22"They came to Bethsaida, and some people brought a blind man and begged Jesus to touch him. 23 He took the blind man by the hand and led him outside the village. When he had spit on the man's eyes and put his hands on him, Jesus asked, "Do you see anything?"24 He looked up and said, "I see people; they look like trees walking around."25 Once more Jesus put his hands on the man's eyes. Then his eyes were opened, his sight was restored, and he saw everything clearly." (NIV)*

I was legally blind in my right eye and my world had become even more depressing with the possibility of losing my sight in both eyes. My yearning for a touch from

God physically and spiritual was crucial if I was to survive. As I lay on my sick bed, my daughter crawled up onto my lap and beheld my face and told me "God gave sight to the blind."

Matthew 21:16 – *"And said unto him, Hearest thou what these say? And Jesus saith unto them, Yea; have ye never read, Out of the mouth of babes and sucklings thou hast perfected praise?"*

Yes, the LORD had used my little 8 year old daughter to speak truth to His power. God can heal us instantly or progressively. I traveled to National Eye Institute (NEI) frequently, always by myself. I was enrolled in a clinical trial, which required numerous visits. God blessed me to be under the care of world-renowned uveitis research doctors whose daily mission was to save the sight of their patients. NEI provided me with sight-saving treatment, reduced my chances of losing my sight, and improved my quality of life.

In 1999, I had my first eye surgery at NEI. Prior to surgery, I had an eye doctor's visit to get my vitals and labs done before surgery. As I sat waiting to have my blood drawn, I became ill and passed out. Once I gained consciousness, I was informed that I have type II diabetes. Long term use of steroidal treatments led to my diabetes. This new diagnosis did not impede the eye surgery to remove the cataracts from my right eye. Surgery was scheduled for the next day.

The cataracts were removed successfully by the skilled hands of my doctor at NEI. Immediately, following surgery, leaving the surgical area, I could see. The faces of the treatment staff were blurry however, I could see again.

Within minutes of entering the recovery area I could see clearly.

Mark 8:24-26 – [24]*"He looked up and said, "I see people; they look like trees walking around."*[25]*Once more Jesus put his hands on the man's eyes. Then his eyes were opened, his sight was restored, and he saw everything clearly.* [26]*Jesus sent him home..." (NIV)*

Journal Entry: July 22, 1999

I can see again. It's like seeing the world for the first time. I believe there is hope at the end of the tunnel. I see the light. With this new gift of sight, I pray to God to let it guide me in the right path. With my new sight, I want to see the spirit and foresee many untold revelations. Thank you God for your healing power. As my daughter said, "God gives sight to the blind." Thank you Jesus. I'm healed.

Not only did God restore my sight, He was restoring my faith. I made it to the doorsteps of Greater Mount Calvary Holy Church (GMCHC) just in the nick of time in 1999. I was famished in my spirit and I needed God to do a miracle in my life physically, spiritually, and emotionally. I needed healing and deliverance. God begin to use Bishop Alfred A. Owens, Jr. to speak truth into my life and GMCHC became my Balm in Gilead. There is healing in the sanctuary. I begin to see and hear God again. I attended GMCHC an entire year in 1999 and I joined the church in January 2000.

I remember meeting with my Pastor, Bishop Owens, and he told me that I had to stop coming to church and sitting in the back and leaving. He told me that I needed to join a ministry and serve. He also was concerned about my emotional needs as well. And, recommended that I receive Christian counseling. As my spiritual father, I took his advice and joined a ministry and started Christian counseling.

The first ministry my family joined was the Junior Voices of Calvary. I had not yet built up my trust with interacting with church folks so I started with my children. This required me to take them to rehearsal on the 4th Saturday of every month, give us an opportunity to fellowship, and build trust. We later joined the Usher Board as a family. While serving the house of the LORD, I heard God's voice instructing me to fulfill my call to ministry. In 2004, I enrolled in Calvary's Bible Institute to be prepared for the ministry. I also served in other ministries in the church.

CHAPTER TWELVE

God My Rod and My Staff

Making my way back to the house of God aligned me with the blessings of God. In January of 2002, I moved from my 2nd apartment to purchasing my first home. I was experiencing success in my career in health communications. My health was manageable. I continued to be monitored by NEI and my physicians for Sarcoidosis, Uveitis, Glaucoma, and Diabetes. I had become a master in managing my chronic diseases.

However, managing my children was becoming more demanding. Both of my children were experiencing learning challenges and needed more of my attention and support. They both were diagnosed with ADHD. I had to advocate and obtain a lawyer for my children to receive an individual education assessment plan (IEP) to meet their educational needs. I was awarded education funding for my daughter to receive tutoring and enrichment programming. My son was awarded funding to attend a day school that specialized in ADHD and other learning disabilities.

By this time in my journey the recession had taken its grip on my household in 2006. My company downsized and I was released from my $68,000 a year job. I was unemployed for six months. During those months of unemployment I volunteered at the church.

I shifted from my first career in health communications to Christian education. God opened a door and closed a door to align me with my destiny. I began to work for the ministry in 2006. After accepting a teaching position at Calvary Christian Academy, I received many job offers to make more money; however, I chose to stay in position and fulfill my God-given assignment.

In 2006, I earned my Certificate in Biblical Studies and in 2007 I earned my Certificate in Ministry from Calvary Bible Institute. In 2007, I became a licensed minister under The Mount Calvary Holy Church of America, Incorporated.

Three years later, my health took a turn for the worse. My vision and body did not bounce back like it did in previous years. I was much older. The cycle of vengeance had now commenced, but my faith was strong, and life's experiences had taught me that this too shall pass.

In 2010, I had emergency glaucoma surgery. My right eye pressure was over 60. At any moment my optic nerve could erupt in my right eye resulting to total blindness. The next day at my post-op visit for the right eye, the doctor informed me that my left eye pressure was extremely high. The eye doctor wanted to do another emergency glaucoma surgery that evening to release the pressure from the left eye. However, I informed the doctor that I had two children at home and I needed to ensure that they would be okay. I went home and immediately sent an email to the Ministerial Alliance asking for prayers for my family and I.

I returned to the hospital the next morning and was prepped for surgery. I was pushed into the cold surgery room. I was on the surgery table and the doctor said, "Let's check her eye pressure one more time." When they checked, my eye pressure in the left eye was within normal range. A miracle had taken place. One of the doctor's on the treatment team stated, "You must have people praying for you. "My response was, "Yes, I do." Then the doctor went on to say that we would not be having surgery that day. God answered our prayers. My family depended on me and having both eyes incapacitated for any length of time was not an option for me. I was a single parent with demanding children, and I had to work. God knows how much we can bear.

James 5:16 – *"Therefore confess your sins to each other and pray for each other so that you may be healed. The prayer of a righteous person is powerful and effective."* *(NIV)*

The aftermath of the high eye pressures in my right eye had left its imprint. As the result of the high eye pressure in the right eye, I lost my peripheral vision. The right eye is at the ending stage of glaucoma. I have lost some vision in my left eye moderately.

Journal Entry: January 11, 2011

As I was commuting from work to home yesterday, I was talking (praying) to God regarding my adjustment to losing my peripheral vision in my right eye and He dropped into my Spirit: "You have wrestled with me and won. I have changed your name." Immediately, Jacob in the Bible came to me as a reference to validate what God had spoken in my Spirit.

Jacob struggled in the night with God, literally (see Genesis 32:22 – 32). At the end of the struggle, Jacob asked for a blessing and was given one:

Genesis 32:28 (NLT)
28 "Your name will no longer be Jacob (Bridget)," the man told him. "From now on you will be called Israel, because you have fought with God and with men and have won."

God Changed My Name...

The summer of 2011, I received orientation and mobility training from the Columbia Light House for the Blind. The training was necessary to help me learn how to navigate my world now that my sight was limited in my right eye. Also, the training was also preparing me for if the day comes that I'm totally blind. My trainer told me everything I'm learning will come back to memory. I had several weeks of intense training. There were periods of depression and anger as I came to the reality that my world had changed. I received my white cane. I'm still in the process of accepting the things that I cannot change.

God grant me the serenity to accept the things I cannot change, the courage to change the things I can, and the wisdom to know the difference.
– Reinhold Niebuhr

I use my cane sometimes. It has been difficult to let go and be vulnerable to allowing God to be my rod and my staff. It is my hope that by sharing my testimony that I will develop the confidence and courage to use my cane daily, until God heals me completely. I desire your prayers.

The cycle of vengeance continued and my eye doctor at NEI prescribed another treatment modality to my already overloaded treatment regimen. The added treatment was for kidney transplant patients; however it is off label use for me. I needed a stronger agent to control the inflammation and to suppress my immune system even more. To no avail, my left eye was compromised in December of 2013. I had glaucoma and cataract surgery to save the sight in my left eye.

My recovery time was lengthy; but it did not stop the miracle. I am healed. I'm being healed. God is a Healer. I am a MIRACLE…

CHAPTER THIRTEEN

My Eyes Dare To Believe

Look at me. I don't look like what I have been through from the time of my conception to now. I'm walking with my rod and staff. My rod is God's strength. My staff is God's Word, His promises and provisions. I call those things that are not as if they are. I am Healed! My Healing is a process and my journey is not over. God inspired me to share my testimony with you and the world to give hope to the downtrodden and those on the margins of life.

God has touched my lips for such a time as this, to not only minister His word on healing and deliverance but to be a living witness. As Bishop Owens says, "It doesn't matter how you feel; God is still worthy to be praised!"

The trials and tribulations that I have endured have made me fall in love with God even more. It has birthed a prayer warrior, a faith walker, and a worshiper of God. My testimony is for real. If God did it for me, He will do it for you.

My prayer is that after reading my book you will be encouraged and "believe beyond what you see." "See GOD and Dare to Believe." All things are possible if you believe God!!! I'm still here because I BELIEVE!!!

My Eyes Dare to Believe,

Minister Bridget P. Robinson

ABOUT THE AUTHOR

Minster Bridget Pershay Robinson is from Columbia, South Carolina. Minister Robinson relocated to Washington, D.C. in the early 90's. Her transition to the metropolitan area is part of God's divine plan for her life. Washington, D.C. provided her with a safe place to build a life for herself and her two children after escaping an abusive marriage. She is the proud mother of a daughter, Hadassah, and a son, Jeffery Fleming. She is also the proud grandmother of Nehemiah Alexander McPherson.

Minister Robinson graduated from the University of the District of Columbia with a Bachelor Degree in Psychology. She earned a Master of Arts Degree in Community Health Promotion and Education from Trinity University. Upon accepting her call into ministry she enrolled into Calvary Bible Institute and received both a Certificate in Biblical Studies and Ministry. She also earned a Certificate of Ministry Leadership from Project Bridges and Regent University.

Minister Robinson has traveled outside of the United States ministering the Word of God. Minister Robinson has had the opportunity to travel to Brazil and minister to the people of Sao, Paulo, Brazil. She ministered at Solid Rock Orphanage of Brazil funded by Pastor Darlene Bishop, local public schools, and the favelas (slums). This experience has provided her with cultural competency to minister globally for the Kingdom of God.

Minister Robinson is a licensed minister under The Mount Calvary Holy Church of America, Inc. (MCHCA). She is an active member of Greater Mount Calvary Holy Church

(GMCHC) and serves on the Ministerial Alliance Board under the leadership of Archbishop Alfred A. Owens, Jr. She is also an educator at Calvary Christian Academy and serves as an instructor at Calvary Bible Institute.

Minister Robinson has a strong background and experience in community outreach and Christian Education. She uses her knowledge gained from her pursuit of higher education and Christian Leadership at GMCHC to empower others to break the chains of abuse by serving men and women who are at the crossroads of life.

My Beloved Sisters and Brothers:

I want to hear from you. Please share with me how the book has empowered and impacted your life. Share your courageous testimony of how you "Dare to Believe God" in spite of what your eyes have seen. You can email me at: myeyesdare2believe@gmail.com. I look forward to hearing from you as we "Dare to Believe God" for His provision, protection, and providence.

I pray God's hands will always be upon you.

Minister Bridget P. Robinson